THE JUNIPER TREE, A TRAGIC HOUSEHOLD TALE

A Musical Play

Written and Composed
By
Wendy Kesselman

SAMUEL FRENCH, INC.

45 West 25th Street
NEW YORK 10010
LONDON

7623 Sunset Boulevard
HOLLYWOOD 90046
TORONTO

ISBN 0 573 61113 0 Printed in U.S.A. #12619

IMPORTANT BILLING AND CREDIT REQUIREMENTS

All producers of *THE JUNIPER TREE, A TRAGIC HOUSEHOLD TALE must* give credit to the Author of the Play in all programs distributed in connection with performances of the Play, and in all instances in which the title of the Play appears for the purposes of advertising, publicizing or otherwise exploiting the Play and /or a production. The name of the Author *must* appear on a separate line on which no other name appears, immediately following the title and *must* appear in size of type not less than fifty percent of the size of the title type.

A Piano/Vocal Score is available for rental from Samuel French upon application.

With special thanks to:

Lyn Austin, Brian Briody, Brenda Currin,
Harwich Junior Theatre, Danny Jenkins,
Inverna Lockpez, Michael McKinstry, Rosalind Pace,
Joanie Patchen, Kim Rust, Nina Schuessler,
Lynda Sturner, Diane Wondisford.

THE JUNIPER TREE was originally produced by the Lenox Arts Center/Music Theatre Group, Lyn Austin, Producing Director, and Lynda Sturner, at Citizen's Hall, Stockbridge, MA, on July 28, 1982. The managing director was Diane Wondisford. The play was directed by Larry Pine, with lighting by William Beautyman.

CAST

First Wife/Stepmother/Marlinchen .... Wendy Kesselman
Husband/Boy...Daniel Jenkins

The play was subsequently produced Off-Broadway at St. Clement's by the Music Theatre/Lenox Arts Center, Lyn Austin, Producing Director, and Playwrights' Forum, Inc., Lynda Sturner, Executive Director, on April 19, 1983. The managing director was Diane Wondisford. It was directed by Michael Montel; the musical director and conceiver was William Schimmel; the set and costumes were by Lawrence Casey; the lighting was by Marilyn Rennagel; and the production stage manager was Robert I. Cohen.

CAST

Narrator/Singer....................... ....Wendy Kesselman
Husband/Boy..Anthony Crivello
First Wife/Stepmother/Marlinchen..............Deborah Offner

MUSICIANS

Conductor/Accordian/Piano.....................William Schimmel
Percussion ....Gary Klein
Clarinet/Bass...Peter Rettegi

CHARACTERS

First Wife (A non-speaking role)
Husband
Stepmother (A non-singing role)
The Boy
Marlinchen
Goldsmith
Goldsmith's Wife
Shoemaker
Miller
Miller's Wife
First Village Child
Second Village Child

PLACE

Under The Juniper Tree

TIME

Two Thousand Years Ago

THE JUNIPER TREE, A TRAGIC HOUSEHOLD TALE is inspired by "The Juniper Tree" from *The Complete Grimm's Fairy Tales* published by Pantheon Books.

MUSICAL NUMBERS

"They Loved Each Other"	*Villagers, First Wife, Husband*
"Ah, If I Had But A Child"	*First Wife*
"If I Die"	*First Wife, Village Children and Women, Husband*
"He Was As Red As Blood"	*Husband, Villagers*
"My Reminder"	*Husband*
"Ah, If I Had But A Child" (Reprise)	*First Wife*
"I Never Had A Name"	*The Boy, Marlinchen*
"So She Took The Little Boy"	*Marlinchen, Children, Villagers*
"Soup"	*Husband, Marlinchen*
"Under The Juniper"	*Marlinchen, Village Children*
"The Bird Flew Away"	*First Wife*
"My Mother She Killed Me"	*Bird (The Boy, Village Children)*
"Under The Juniper" (Reprise)	*Company*
"Finale"	*Company*

PRODUCTION NOTES

The play will benefit from the simplest production values. A bare raked stage with a scrim at the back, behind which, at times, we see the juniper tree, and through which the First Wife can emerge. A brown steamer trunk, which doubles as a table. Two apples. A black soup pot and black spoon. A large white handkerchief, which doubles as a tablecloth. And the actors, barefoot, simply costumed in black and white.

The play is performed without an intermission.

The ideal instruments are piano, flute, guitar, cello and violin. The play can be performed with piano alone. If desired, a gobo of the bird can be used to startling effect, but the bird itself should be performed by the Boy and the two Village Children.

In this publication of THE JUNIPER TREE, A TRAGIC HOUSEHOLD TALE, there are twelve actors. However, the cast can be made up of anywhere from two to twenty actors. Two actors would play all the roles, including the Bird, sung by them both. Different effects will be gained with whatever the number of actors chosen.

for Brian

THE JUNIPER TREE, A TRAGIC HOUSEHOLD TALE

Darkness. Before light comes up, the first notes of "They Loved Each Other" are heard.

Light comes up on the VILLAGERS and VILLAGE CHILDREN on a bare raked stage.

"They Loved Each Other"

FIRST VILLAGE CHILD

(Sings)

IT IS NOW LONG AGO

SECOND VILLAGE CHILD

(Sings)

TWO THOUSAND YEARS AGO

FIRST VILLAGE CHILD

THAT THERE WAS A RICH MAN WHO HAD

SECOND VILLAGE CHILD

A BEAUTIFUL

FIRST VILLAGE CHILD

HE HAD A BEAUTIFUL

VILLAGE CHILDREN

HE HAD A BEAUTIFUL AND PIOUS WIFE

VILLAGERS, VILLAGE CHILDREN

(Sing)

AND THEY LOVED EACH OTHER DEARLY
THEY LOVED EACH OTHER DEARLY
AND THEY LOVED EACH OTHER
THEY LOVED EACH OTHER
THEY LOVED EACH OTHER DEARLY

MILLER'S WIFE
AND THEY HUGGED EACH OTHER DAILY

MILLER
AND THEY KISSED EACH OTHER FREQUENTLY

VILLAGERS, VILLAGE CHILDREN
AND THEY HUGGED EACH OTHER
THEY KISSED EACH OTHER
THEY KISSED EACH OTHER FREQUENTLY

GOLDSMITH'S WIFE
(Overlapping)
AND THEY FED EACH OTHER EVERY BITE

GOLDSMITH
AND THEY TICKLED EACH OTHER EVERY NIGHT

VILLAGERS, VILLAGE CHILDREN
THEY FED EACH OTHER
THEY TICKLED EACH OTHER
THEY TICKLED EACH OTHER —

(Light comes up on the FIRST WIFE and the HUSBAND)

FIRST WIFE
(Sings)
AND THEY LOVED EACH OTHER DEARLY

HUSBAND
(Sings)
THEY LOVED EACH OTHER DEARLY

HUSBAND and FIRST WIFE
AND THEY LOVED EACH OTHER
THEY LOVED EACH OTHER

HUSBAND
THEY LOVED EACH OTHER —

FIRST WIFE

IT IS NOW LONG AGO
TWO THOUSAND YEARS AGO. . .

HUSBAND

I wanted to tell you about the first time I saw her. It was one of those winter days when everything is very pure and very still. A tremendous snowfall had been going on the last several days. The whole forest was *thick* with snow. It was. . . extraordinary. I was coming home, walking along, when something started appearing to me out of the snow. At first I thought it was a tree moving in the forest. . . but then I realized it was coming closer. And it was a great white horse coming toward me, a great white horse that looked as if it had. . . *emerged* almost — out of the snow. And on the horse, there was a woman. . . a child. And it was her skin that was the most amazing thing because it was like. . . she had been *born* that day. It was so white. And this red, red mouth. She rode by me, but for weeks I couldn't get the vision of that horse and that face out of my mind. Finally I decided to find out who she was. She was poor. She came from a poor family. And that was a problem. Because our family had always been rich. But I knew I had to have her. My parents were completely opposed to the marriage. But I married her. I think the only thing that consoled them was the possibility of a son. An heir.

(*A moment)*

And that, curiously enough, was the one thing that didn't happen.

FIRST WIFE

AND THEY LOVED EACH OTHER DEARLY

HUSBAND

BUT THEY DIDN'T HAVE ANY CHILDREN

FIRST WIFE

NO THEY DIDN'T HAVE ANY

HUSBAND
THEY DIDN'T HAVE ANY

FIRST WIFE and HUSBAND
THEY DIDN'T HAVE ANY CHILDREN

FIRST WIFE
AND THEY HUGGED EACH OTHER DAILY

HUSBAND
(Whirling her around in a dance)
AND THEY KISSED EACH OTHER FREQUENTLY

FIRST WIFE
AND THEY FED EACH OTHER EVERY BITE

HUSBAND
AND THEY TICKLED EACH OTHER EVERY NIGHT
THEY HUGGED

FIRST WIFE
THEY KISSED

FIRST WIFE and HUSBAND
THEY TICKLED EACH OTHER. . .
BUT THEY DIDN'T HAVE ANY CHILDREN

FIRST WIFE
BUT THEY LOVED EACH OTHER DEARLY

HUSBAND
BUT THEY DIDN'T HAVE ANY CHILDREN

FIRST WIFE and HUSBAND
OH THEY LOVED EACH OTHER
THEY LOVED EACH OTHER
BUT THEY DIDN'T HAVE ANY CHILDREN

HUSBAND

I mean it wasn't that we weren't very happy together. We were! She was a delightful person. Very ethereal. And a great believer. Her whole family was like that. And of course my family had been atheists *forever.* Money is their only god. Her belief touched me in a way. And yet there was this. . . unattainable quality about her. . . the same thing I felt out there in the snow, the very thing I wanted — it was like I could never really. . . get that.

(He pauses, as light comes up on the juniper tree)

There was a big tree out in the courtyard. A juniper tree. Immense. Twisted. Dark dark green. There was something oddly comforting about that tree. She began spending more and more time out there. She was always there.

(Softer, as the music begins under)

It was snowing. And she stood under the juniper tree, with an apple in one hand and a knife in the other, paring and paring away. Suddenly she *cut* herself with the knife. And I saw blood. . . fall on the snow. And I heard her moan.

"Ah, If I Had But A Child"

FIRST WIFE

AH, IF I HAD BUT A CHILD
AS RED AS BLOOD
AND AS WHITE AS SNOW

AH, IF I HAD BUT A CHILD
AS RED AS BLOOD
AND AS WHITE AS SNOW

AH, IF I HAD BUT A CHILD

HUSBAND

(Overlapping on "child")

I had never seen her bleed. There was something so white and perfect about her that to see blood coming out of her startled me, *woke* something in me I never felt before. I rushed outside and kind of gathered her up and was about to take her back into the house when. . . I just lay down with her. In the snow — like that — I lay down with her.

"If I Die"

FIRST WIFE

AND A MONTH WENT BY
AND THE SNOW WAS GONE
AND TWO MONTHS
AND THEN EVERYTHING WAS GREEN
AND THREE MONTHS
AND THEN ALL THE FLOWERS CAME OUT
OF THE EARTH
AND FOUR MONTHS
AND ALL THE TREES IN THE WOOD GREW
THICKER
AND THE GREEN BRANCHES WERE ALL
CLOSELY ENTWINED

AND THE BIRDS SANG
AND ALL THE WOOD RESOUNDED
AND THE BLOSSOMS FELL FROM THE TREES

AND THE BIRDS SANG
AND ALL THE WOOD RESOUNDED
AND THE BLOSSOMS FELL FROM THE TREES

(Ecstatic, the HUSBAND kisses the FIRST WIFE, moves away, watching her from a distance)

FIRST WIFE

THEN THE FIFTH MONTH PASSED AWAY
AND SHE STOOD UNDER THE JUNIPER TREE
WHICH SMELT SO SWEETLY
THAT HER HEART LEAPT
AND SHE FELL ON HER KNEES
AND WAS BESIDE HERSELF WITH JOY

AND SHE FELL ON HER KNEES
AND WAS BESIDE HERSELF WITH JOY

AND WHEN THE SIXTH MONTH WAS OVER
THE FRUIT WAS LARGE AND FINE
AND WHEN THE SIXTH MONTH WAS OVER

THE FRUIT WAS LARGE AND FINE
AND WHEN THE SIXTH MONTH WAS OVER
THE FRUIT WAS LARGE AND FINE

(The VILLAGE CHILDREN appear)

VILLAGE CHILDREN
AND THEN SHE WAS QUITE STILL
AND THEN SHE WAS QUITE STILL
AND THEN SHE WAS
SHE WAS QUITE STILL

(The VILLAGE WOMEN appear)

VILLAGE CHILDREN and WOMEN
AND THEN SHE WAS
QUITE STILL

(The HUSBAND steps forward)

HUSBAND, VILLAGE WOMEN, CHILDREN
AND THE SEVENTH MONTH SHE SNATCHED
AT THE JUNIPER BERRIES
AND ATE THEM GREEDILY
THEN SHE GREW SICK AND SORROWFUL

VILLAGE CHILDREN
THEN SHE GREW SICK AND SORROWFUL

VILLAGE WOMEN
THEN THE EIGHT MONTH PASSED
AND SHE CALLED HER HUSBAND TO HER

HUSBAND, VILLAGE WOMEN, CHILDREN
(As the WOMEN and CHILDREN go out)
AND WEPT AND SAID

FIRST WIFE

IF I DIE
THEN BURY ME
IF I DIE
THEN BURY ME
IF I DIE
THEN BURY ME
BENEATH THE JUNIPER TREE

FIRST WIFE and HUSBAND

IF I DIE
THEN BURY ME
IF I DIE
THEN BURY ME
IF I DIE
THEN BURY ME
BENEATH THE JUNIPER TREE

IF I DIE
THEN BURY ME
BENEATH THE JUNIPER TREE

HUSBAND

Well. . . anyway, I buried her. And I *did* bury her under the juniper tree. It was completely against the family's wishes. That was unheard of — burying somebody under a tree. We all had. . . *plots*. But she wanted it that way. She had been so strange during her pregnancy. The juniper seemed to become a tremendous thing for her. Maybe because that's where it happened. I felt as if our life began under the tree. Because of the tree.

(He pauses)

I had been very strong until that point. And then. . . it was a year I thought I'd never get through. Because I kept having that *vision*, that first vision of her on the white horse, coming out of the snow. And of course I had the *boy*. . . who was so much like her. Whenever I saw him, I would see. . . He was a constant reminder.

(A pause)

Until I met her.

(Light comes up on the STEPMOTHER)

STEPMOTHER

GOD. After she died. . . I thought he would lose his mind. I mean you really had to feel sorry for him. And I did. I did feel sorry for him. As a matter of fact I felt so sorry I went over and asked if I could help out. He didn't say anything when I asked. He just sat there under that tree. So. . . I just started in. I figured if he'd mind he'd tell me.

(A moment)

There was this baby. This beautiful baby. Lying in a wooden cradle. Still. . . still as a mouse. Watching me with these huge eyes. Looking at me all the time. And he. . . the father. . . he fascinated me. *God*, he just fascinated me. So I went over every day and cleaned the house and helped with the baby. And then one day I told him I was leaving early because there was a dance that night.

HUSBAND

(Looking up)

A dance?

STEPMOTHER

Oh, just a country dance. Nothing you'd —

(Sucking in her breath)

And then I realized it was the first, the very first time he'd shown any interest in *anything*, since that wife of his died. And I asked if he wanted to come along. He didn't look like much of a dancer to me. But I didn't care. I walked ahead of him through the grass. I was wearing this *bright* red dress I had made and I could just feel him looking at me. I was almost scared to turn around and see his face. But all I wanted to do was turn around.

(As the GOLDSMITH and MILLER appear, and a guitar and violin play)

It was nearly dark when we got there and right away someone asked me to dance.

(As she dances with each of the men)

I saw him standing on the side. . . watching me, watching me, not dancing with anyone. I danced with *everyone*. I knew he saw me laugh up at them, touch the curve of their necks, put my hands on their shoulders. And I wanted him to see it. Finally, breathless and hot, the sweat pouring down my arms, my red dress sticking to me, I went and stood in front of him. "Come on. Let's go for a walk. I can see you don't want to dance." And he put his arm around my shoulders and we walked through the fields. And I could feel the low grass wet on my ankles and the high grass wet on my thighs and I could feel myself growing wetter and wetter just from walking beside him. There was no moon that night. But he seemed to know exactly where he was going. And he took his hand from my shoulder and grabbed my hand, and pulled, just pulled me along. And then he pushed me down on my knees and got down on his knees beside me and we crawled along on our hands and knees and suddenly the earth grew warm, very warm and very soft.

(As a faint light illuminates the juniper tree)

The branches came so low they touched my hands when I touched him. The leaves caught in my hair. I tasted the bark with my tongue. And when he cried out. . . an even louder, more piercing cry rose from the house. It was the baby. But I placed my hands on his ears and rolled him back on the earth and pressed myself against him with the branches of the tree bruising me, and I wanted it that way, I wanted it that way, I wanted it till the sound of our breathing was all that was left.

(Light comes up on the MILLER'S WIFE)

"He Was As Red As Blood"

MILLER'S WIFE

BY THE SECOND WIFE HE HAD A DAUGHTER
BUT THE FIRST WIFE'S CHILD WAS A LITTLE SON
AND HE WAS AS RED AS BLOOD
AND AS WHITE AS SNOW

(The other VILLAGERS appear)

VILLAGERS

BY THE SECOND WIFE HE HAD A DAUGHTER

BUT THE FIRST WIFE'S CHILD WAS A LITTLE SON
AND HE WAS AS RED AS BLOOD
AND AS WHITE AS SNOW

(Light comes up on the young BOY, rushing awkwardly to sit between his father and the STEPMOTHER)

HUSBAND

AND HE WAS AS RED AS BLOOD
AND AS WHITE AS SNOW
AND HE WAS AS RED AS BLOOD
AND AS WHITE AS SNOW

HUSBAND, VILLAGERS

AND HE WAS AS RED AS BLOOD
AND HE WAS AS RED AS BLOOD
AND HE WAS AS RED AS BLOOD
AND AS WHITE. . .

"My Reminder"

HUSBAND

SO MUCH LIKE HER
OH JUST LIKE HER
(As the VILLAGERS go off)
A CERTAIN SMILE
A CERTAIN LOOK
EVEN THE WAY HE READS A BOOK
EVEN THE WAY HE SHUTS A DOOR
AND SHE'S BEFORE ME
HOW SHE ADORES ME
(As the FIRST WIFE appears in the juniper tree, comes toward him)
SHE LIFTS HER ARMS
SHE LIFTS HER FACE
AND I AM LOST IN HER EMBRACE
THAT TENDER MOUTH
THOSE DREAMING EYES
AND WE ARE FLYING
OR AM I DYING

(Whirling around with her)
TO DIE BENEATH THE TREE
AH, THAT WOULD BE SUBLIME NOW
BUT NEVER, NOT FOR ME
ANOTHER LIFE IS MINE NOW
(Slower)
AND A NEW WIFE. . . IS MINE NOW
(He is still, as the STEPMOTHER takes his hand, smiles up at him)
AND THEN A WORD
AND THEN A PHRASE
HIS SUDDEN LAUGH
HIS SECRET GAZE
I SHUT MY EYES
REACH OUT MY HAND
AND SO I FIND HER
THROUGH MY REMINDER
CONSTANT REMINDER. . .

(The FIRST WIFE appears behind him, covers his eyes with her hands. And once again the music soars as he sweeps her into the dance)

FIRST WIFE
(Finally breaking away)
AH, IF I HAD BUT A CHILD

HUSBAND
AND THEN A WORD
AND THEN A PHRASE
HIS SUDDEN LAUGH
HIS SECRET GAZE

FIRST WIFE
AH, IF I HAD BUT A CHILD
AS RED AS BLOOD

HUSBAND	**FIRST WIFE**
I CLOSE MY EYES	AH, AS RED AS BLOOD
HOLD OUT MY HAND	AH, AS RED AS BLOOD

AND SO I FIND HER
THROUGH MY REMINDER
CONSTANT REMINDER

AND AS WHITE
AS WHITE
AS SNOW

HUSBAND

HE'S MY REMINDER
SO I REMEMBER. . .

(MARLINCHEN appears, stands behind the STEPMOTHER, as a trunk is brought in by the MILLER and GOLDSMITH)

MARLINCHEN

(Sings)

BY THE SECOND WIFE HE HAD A DAUGHTER. . .

BOY

I remember when they had Marlinchen.

MARLINCHEN

(Swooping toward him, grabbing him from behind the neck)

I used to wish he was my real brother.

BOY

There was a big storm that night. I was up in my room, and the juniper tree, where my real mother is buried, was banging against the window.

(As light comes up on a rapid image of the FIRST WIFE in the juniper tree)

Every time my stepmother screamed, I reached out and held onto its branches.

MARLINCHEN

I tried to get him to talk about his real mother. But he wouldn't. Sometimes a whole day would go by and he'd say one sentence. But sometimes that sentence would be really important. Like when he told me about the look on her face. The happy look when she died.

(Turning to the BOY)

But how can you remember that? You'd just been born.

(She pauses, looking out)
He smiled at me. That secret smile.

BOY

The next morning, when they showed her to me, I felt so happy, I couldn't wait for her to be my friend.

MARLINCHEN

I used to love to look at him. He had the best face. I'd sit and watch him for hours. I couldn't call him anything. Because he didn't have a name. She died before she had a chance to name him. But that didn't matter. Because looking at him was the best part. My mother *hated* when I did that.

BOY

Even when she was really little she knew all about everything. She wasn't scared of a thing.

MARLINCHEN

But she couldn't scare *me*. The only thing I didn't like. . . she had these secrets. Always. All these things she wouldn't tell us about.

(She pauses)

Like she had this trunk. This big trunk up in the attic. It was kind of brown and, I don't know, funny looking, but I was just *dying* to look inside. And she wouldn't let us go near it. That drove me crazy. Because I really wanted to see what was in there. I mean I really wanted to.

(Running to the trunk)

Let's look!

BOY

You look.

MARLINCHEN

No you. You go first.

BOY

No.

MARLINCHEN

Yes.

BOY

No.

MARLINCHEN

Yes.

BOY

(emphatic)

No.

MARLINCHEN

Okay, okay. I'll look.

(She opens the trunk)

Oooh. *Oooh.*

(They both stare inside)

BOY

There're so many.

MARLINCHEN

Let's take one.

BOY

No.

MARLINCHEN

Yes.

BOY

No.

MARLINCHEN

(Taking an apple from the trunk)

Yes!

(She sits on the trunk)

Why're you so worried about her all the time? What she's gonna do, what she's gonna think?

(Polishing the apple)

I don't care *what* she thinks.

(He smiles)

BOY

(Suddenly anxious)

Are you sure she won't come up here?

MARLINCHEN

Positive.

BOY

Really?

(MARLINCHEN nods)

Go look, Marlinchen — would you?

(As MARLINCHEN spits on the apple, polishes it with a fervor)

Please.

(Totally engrossed, MARLINCHEN continues polishing the apple)

Please.

(With a reassuring smile, MARLINCHEN thrusts the apple into his hand, runs out.

The BOY draws the apple to his face, smells it. A blissful smile, as light comes up on the STEPMOTHER)

STEPMOTHER

The trouble was. . . nothing he did was ever quite right. Marlinchen did everything wrong. But it didn't matter with her. It was him. It was the boy. I couldn't *stand* it if he made a mistake.

(Turning to the BOY, who sits on the trunk, carefully polishing the apple)

What are you doing up here?

(Quickly he hides the apple)

STEPMOTHER

(Quiet)

I've told you never. . . never to come up here, haven't I?

(Silence)

Where's Marlinchen?

(Still silence)
I thought she was with you.
(Coming closer)
You look so sweet with your hair like that.
(Gently taking his hair in her hand, lightly pulling back his head. Soft)
Just like her.
(*Quickly releasing his hair)*
You don't have to be scared of me. Please don't be scared of me.
(Bending over him, her face next to his)
Please.
(Sucking the air in between her teeth)
What have you got in your hand?
(He is still)
One of my apples, isn't it?
(He doesn't respond)
Isn't it?
(He remains silent)
Answer me!

(She pulls his hand forward, wrenches the apple away. Staring at him, she goes off.

The BOY gazes out at us, not breathing. Utter stillness.

A faint moan escapes him. He shuts his lips, draws his knees close together. Tears come to his eyes. He forces them back, shuts his eyes tight. The tears slip down.

Music of "My Reminder" under, as suddenly he leaps up, runs to the juniper tree. He lies beneath it, his face pressed to the earth)

MARLINCHEN

(Hurrying in, out of breath)

Where were you? I've been looking for you everywhere.

(He doesn't answer)

Where's that apple?

(Laughing)

I was sure it would be gone by now.

(There is no response. She takes a step closer. Quiet)

Did anything happen up there? In. . . in the attic I mean?

(Still silence)

Tell me.

(Soft)

You can *tell me.*

(Softer)

Really.

(Not a sound escapes the BOY. He lies still, almost clinging to the earth)

MARLINCHEN

(Leaning over him, gentle)

Do you feel anything?

(Lying down too)

Do you?

BOY

(His voice choked)

What?

MARLINCHEN

Her bones. Moving.

BOY

Bones? Her bones must be gone by now.

MARLINCHEN

Oh no. I feel them. Don't you feel them?

(The BOY lies quiet, not moving)

Don't you?

BOY

(A sudden laugh)

Oh. I feel it! I feel it. That's not her bones, dummy. It's her heart. Still going.

MARLINCHEN

(A huge intake of breath)

You're right.

"I Never Had A Name"

BOY

I NEVER HAD A NAME
SHE NEVER GAVE ME ONE
NOT THAT SHE WAS TO BLAME
WHAT'S DONE IS DONE

SOMETIMES I LIE AWAKE
WISHING I COULD DECIDE
WHAT THE NAME WAS SHE WOULD HAVE
NAMED ME
BEFORE SHE DIED

(Standing up, moving away)

SOMETIMES I'M LATE FOR SCHOOL
SOMETIMES I LOSE MY WAY
SOMETIMES THAT'S ALL I THINK ABOUT
EVERY DAY

MARLINCHEN

(Moving toward him)

IF YOU ARE LATE FOR SCHOOL
WHY DON'T YOU LOSE YOUR WAY
I KNOW A PLACE THAT WE CAN HIDE IN
EVERY DAY
SOMEWHERE THE LEAVES GROW THICK

MARLINCHEN and BOY

SOMEWHERE THE MOON WILL SHINE
SOMEWHERE THE BERRIES TASTE SO BITTER
JUST LIKE WINE

DEEP IN THE JUNIPER
DEEP IN THE DARK DARK GREEN
WE CAN DO ANYTHING WE WANT TO
WE WON'T BE SEEN

BOY

I NEVER HAD A NAME
MAYBE WITH YOU I CAN
MAYBE DEEP WITHIN ITS BRANCHES
I'LL UNDERSTAND

MARLINCHEN

YOU NEVER HAD A NAME
BUT I KNOW WITH ME
YOU CAN
WE WON'T GIVE UP
UNTIL WE FIND IT
COME, TAKE MY HAND

BOY

I NEVER HAD A NAME
MAYBE WITH YOU
I CAN
MAYBE DEEP
WITHIN ITS BRANCHES
I'LL UNDERSTAND

MARLINCHEN and BOY

WE WON'T GIVE UP UNTIL WE FIND IT
COME, TAKE MY HAND

(MARLINCHEN stands still, her hand outstretched.

The BOY gazes at her, suddenly laughs, takes her hand.

They run off, as light comes up on the HUSBAND and STEPMOTHER)

HUSBAND

There was a dream I began having

STEPMOTHER

I began having this dream

HUSBAND

Every night almost

STEPMOTHER
(Overlapping on "almost")
Almost every night

HUSBAND
But I couldn't tell her about it

STEPMOTHER
I couldn't tell him about it

(The flute plays "If I Die")

HUSBAND
Because my first wife was in it.

STEPMOTHER
Because it was about his first wife.

HUSBAND
That vision still haunted me.

STEPMOTHER
That white skin. That red red mouth. Just like. . . him.

HUSBAND
Once again it nearly drove me mad.

STEPMOTHER
Like. . . the boy.

HUSBAND
In the dark

STEPMOTHER
(Overlapping on "dark")
In the dark

HUSBAND	**STEPMOTHER**
It was terrifying	It was terrifying

HUSBAND
Her heart beating under my hand

STEPMOTHER
Her heart beating under that tree

(The flute stops)

HUSBAND	**STEPMOTHER**
Her heartbeat	Her heartbeat

HUSBAND
And I clung to her

STEPMOTHER
(Overlapping on "her")
I clung to him

HUSBAND	**STEPMOTHER**
Praying	Praying

STEPMOTHER
Things would be different in the morning

HUSBAND
(Overlapping on "in the morning")
In the morning things would be different

STEPMOTHER
He wouldn't look at me that way

HUSBAND
That way he had of looking at her

STEPMOTHER
The boy I mean

HUSBAND
My son I mean

STEPMOTHER	**HUSBAND**
That scared look	That scared look

STEPMOTHER

As if I had

HUSBAND

As if he had

STEPMOTHER	**HUSBAND**
Done something wrong	Done something wrong

HUSBAND

That scared look as if she might

STEPMOTHER

As if I might

HUSBAND	**STEPMOTHER**
I don't know — *hit* him!	I don't know — *hit* him!

(They pause)

HUSBAND

Her arms around me blotted out his face

STEPMOTHER

His arms around me blotted out the boy,

HUSBAND

And in the morning. . . her caresses. . .

STEPMOTHER

Blotted out the morning when I woke him up for school

HUSBAND

The way she touched me

STEPMOTHER

I hated that he touched me, that he reached me, when I watched him swinging his schoolbag on the way home. . . meandering, meandering.

HUSBAND
If she could touch me that way

STEPMOTHER
Why did he have to look at me that way? As if I could give him the world.

HUSBAND
If she could touch me, how could she

STEPMOTHER
And even if he reached the innermost part of me — his loneliness — did that mean I had to

HUSBAND
"No," I told myself. I had to be dreaming.

STEPMOTHER
"No," I told myself. "No."

HUSBAND
That can't be.

STEPMOTHER
That must not be.

HUSBAND
Never. She wouldn't.

STEPMOTHER
But it was as if something drove me

HUSBAND
I'm creating some monster

STEPMOTHER
Just drove me

HUSBAND
As if by magic words I could create magic events

STEPMOTHER

Though I closed off my ears

HUSBAND

As if by a sudden thought

STEPMOTHER

And held back my hands

HUSBAND

A glance over my shoulder

STEPMOTHER

And bit my tongue

HUSBAND

A coming into a room by accident, I could see it happening, I could make it happen.

(He goes out as light reveals the BOY)

STEPMOTHER

(Overlapping on "happen")

I had to, I had to, I had to.

(Slapping the BOY)

You little monster!

(He falls to the floor)

You think you own this house, don't you? Just like *her*.

(Hitting him)

I hate you. I hate you. God, I hate you!

(For an instant the BOY turns, stares out at us, trembling all over, turns back)

Oh God, look what you're doing to me. Look what you're making me do. This isn't me. It's you. You.

(Crying helplessly)

I'm not like this. I'm not.

(Moving closer)

Don't you know I love you? I love you. Don't you know that?

(Shaking, he doesn't respond)

You're driving me crazy!

(Tears streaming down her face)

Please. Please. Say something. Don't you see I want you to talk to me? Please. *Speak*! You're killing me. I beg you. Talk to me. Just talk to me.

(He does not breathe. She turns away, stands beneath the juniper tree, her back to us, as the BOY turns out)

BOY

She was everywhere. There wasn't one place I could go without her being there. Even the juniper tree. She hated that tree. She wanted it cut down, chopped up for firewood.

(A quick pause)

But sometimes she was so much fun. She'd make up all these great games we'd play. And tell us all these fantastic stories. And it was always fine. . . except when I was alone with her. Then it would start out fine, but it would end up terrible. I always did something wrong. Something that got her really mad. So sometimes she'd. . .

(Very soft, fast)

hit me. But only just a little.

(Louder)

And sometimes. . . well, sometimes she could be so sweet. Especially when we made up. Those were the best times. And then everything would be fine again. Until the next time.

(Light comes up on MARLINCHEN and the STEPMOTHER)

STEPMOTHER

Sometimes I think if it hadn't been for Marlinchen none of this would have happened. Because when I came upstairs, there she was, sitting right on top of the trunk. *Right* where she wasn't supposed to be. And right away, as soon as she saw me —

MARLINCHEN

(Sings)

MOTHER, GIVE ME AN APPLE
MOTHER, GIVE ME AN APPLE

STEPMOTHER

'Yes. Of course you can have an apple.' And I gave her this *bright* red apple. But to get the apple, I had to lift the lid of the trunk. And when I lifted up the lid, I suddenly realized how heavy it was.

(As a high-pitched flute plays under)

And how sharp.

MARLINCHEN

(Sings)

MOTHER, IS BROTHER NOT TO HAVE ONE TOO?
MOTHER, IS BROTHER NOT TO HAVE ONE TOO?

STEPMOTHER

I don't know why that made me so angry. *Really* angry. It made me *furious* in fact. And I said,

(She half speaks, half sings)

'YES, WHEN HE COMES HOME FROM SCHOOL.
YES, WHEN HE COMES HOME FROM SCHOOL.'

(The BOY appears. Daydreaming, he meanders along the edge of the stage)

STEPMOTHER

And just then I looked out the window, and there he was. Meandering along as usual, with that long blue scarf, those little shoes. Meandering, meandering. And something happened to me just then. It was like —

(Breathing in)

I don't know — like something got right in*side* me and I *grabbed* the apple away from Marlinchen,

(She half speaks, half sings)

YOU SHALL NOT HAVE ONE
BEFORE YOUR BROTHER
YOU SHALL NOT HAVE ONE
BEFORE YOUR BROTHER

(She throws the apple into the trunk, closes the lid, as MARLINCHEN goes out)

And I threw the apple into the trunk.

(A pause)

And then he came in. Then he was standing right in front of me, looking at me with those huge eyes.

(She half speaks, half sings)

OH WON'T YOU HAVE AN APPLE, MY SON?
OH WON'T YOU HAVE AN APPLE, MY SON?

BOY

Mother, how terrible you look!

(Sings)

BUT YES, I'D LIKE AN APPLE, MOTHER
YES, I'D LIKE AN APPLE, MOTHER

STEPMOTHER

And it was as if something *forced* me to say,

(Deep)

'Well then, come. Just come with me.' And I lifted up the lid of the trunk.

(She half speaks, half sings)

TAKE THE APPLE OUT FOR YOURSELF
TAKE THE APPLE OUT FOR YOURSELF

(With a surprised smile, the BOY comes closer)

And as he was stooping, as he bent down, that same thing pushed me, it told me, it said,

(Sucking in her breath)

It made me, it made me, it just made me do it, and I — I —

(CRASH! She slams down the lid of the trunk.

Abruptly, the light changes, as the BOY freezes in an attitude of shock)

STEPMOTHER

And his head flew off and fell among the red apples. His head flew off and fell among the red apples.

(Moaning)

Ohh. Ohh. Ohh.

(Pause)

If only I could make them think it was not done by me.

(In a rush)

So. . . I went upstairs to my chest of drawers, and I took a white handkerchief out of the top drawer, and I set the head on the neck again —

(As she sets the head on the neck of the BOY)

And I folded the handkerchief so that nothing could be seen —

(She wraps the handkerchief around his neck)

And I sat him on a chair in front of the door, and put an apple in his hand.

(She thrusts an apple in his hand, goes out, as MARLINCHEN runs in, slides onto the trunk beside the BOY)

MARLINCHEN

I thought he was playing a game with me.

(Turning to him)

Give it to me. C'mon. Give me the apple. And take that silly white handkerchief off your neck.

(He remains silent, immobile, as the STEPMOTHER comes in with a large black pot and black spoon to prepare dinner)

Come on! Give it to me.

(Frustrated, she runs to her mother)

STEPMOTHER

I knew exactly what she was going to say the minute she came in.

MARLINCHEN

(Sings)

MOTHER, BROTHER IS SITTING AT THE DOOR
MOTHER, BROTHER IS SITTING AT THE DOOR

STEPMOTHER

But I couldn't speak, I couldn't speak.

MARLINCHEN

He looks so white, Mother, and he's got this apple in his hand.

STEPMOTHER

What could I say, what could I say to her?

MARLINCHEN

I asked him to give it to me. But he wouldn't answer me. I was so scared, Mother. So scared.

STEPMOTHER

Well, go back to him, and if he doesn't answer you this time, give him a box on the ear.

(A moment)

And I began stirring a pot of water on the stove,

(She stirs, as MARLINCHEN goes back and sits on the trunk beside the BOY)

Stirring faster and faster, and then humming, louder and louder.

(She hums, as MARLINCHEN silently coaxes the BOY, who remains still. Finally, she lightly taps his ear.

The apple falls out of his hand and rolls down to the edge of the stage)

MARLINCHEN

(Rushing to her mother)

Mother, Mother, I went back to him and I — I —

STEPMOTHER

(Stirring, overlapping)

I didn't want to hear it, I didn't want to.

MARLINCHEN

(Overlapping)

'BROTHER, GIVE ME THE APPLE,' I SAID
'BROTHER, GIVE ME THE APPLE'
but he wouldn't answer me. He wouldn't! So I — I —

STEPMOTHER

(Stirring and stirring)

I won't listen. I won't!

MARLINCHEN

(Wailing)

On his ear, Mother, on his ear.

(Making a fist and punching out)

And his head, Mother! His head. . .

(She weeps)

STEPMOTHER

And then I knew it had happened. It happened just as I thought it would, because she had done just what I told her to do. And I gathered her up in my arms, and I rocked her.

MARLINCHEN

She told me it would be a secret. A secret just between us.

(She pauses)

But what about Daddy?

STEPMOTHER

No! Not Daddy. You mustn't ever tell Daddy.

MARLINCHEN

Why not?

STEPMOTHER

Well. . . we don't want Daddy to get upset, do we?

MARLINCHEN

No.

STEPMOTHER

So don't tell. If you don't, I won't.

MARLINCHEN

Oh, I won't. I'd be afraid to tell Daddy.

STEPMOTHER

You don't have to. There's no reason to.

MARLINCHEN
But. . . what are we going to do?

STEPMOTHER
(At a loss)
What do we usually do?

MARLINCHEN
(After a pause)
I don't know — make dinner?

STEPMOTHER
(After a pause)
That's right.
(Another pause, thinking)
That's right. Make dinner.

MARLINCHEN
But what are we going to have?

STEPMOTHER
Guess. I'll give you *three* guesses.

(Light comes up on the HUSBAND)

HUSBAND
(Waking up)
I fell asleep after lunch. And I had this nice long dream. We were all sitting under the juniper tree. . .
(As a chord plays under)
Having a picnic.

MARLINCHEN
Pot roast!

STEPMOTHER
No.

HUSBAND
One of those picnics I'd always dreamed of having —

(Another chord under)

You know, with the napkins so white and luxurious and the tablecloth spread out on the grass.

MARLINCHEN

Spaghetti with clam sauce!

STEPMOTHER

No.

HUSBAND

It had such a peaceful feeling, that dream.

(Another chord)

That tender sleepy feeling when you don't want to wake up.

STEPMOTHER

Guess again. You only have one more guess.

HUSBAND

There were all these wonderful little delicacies in the picnic hamper.

STEPMOTHER

Guess.

HUSBAND

Cold chicken and cold turkey and those thin thin cucumber sandwiches with the ends of the bread cut off.

MARLINCHEN

And then I knew. I knew what she was talking about. But I couldn't let her do it alone. Because she was crying even more than I was. And it always scared me when she cried.

HUSBAND

And when we had laid everything out on the white tablecloth, we held hands and said this sort of prayer.

(Another chord under)

MARLINCHEN

I tried not to get under her feet. She was always telling me I got under her feet. But this time — maybe because of what she had to do — maybe she was glad I was there.

HUSBAND

And the sun shone down through the leaves of the juniper and blessed the food

(Chord under "blessed the food")

we were about to eat.

"So She Took The Little Boy"

MARLINCHEN

SO SHE TOOK THE LITTLE BOY
AND CHOPPED HIM INTO PIECES
PUT HIM IN THE PAN
AND MADE HIM INTO SOUP

OH SHE TOOK THE LITTLE BOY
AND CHOPPED HIM INTO PIECES
PUT HIM IN THE PAN
AND MADE HIM INTO SOUP

(The VILLAGE CHILDREN appear, start a game of pat-a-cake upstage, as MARLINCHEN and the STEPMOTHER, downstage, make the soup)

MARLINCHEN, VILLAGE CHILDREN

BUT MARLINCHEN STOOD BY
WEEPING AND WEEPING
THINKING IT WAS ALL HER FAULT
AND HER TEARS FELL INTO THE PAN SO THAT
THERE WAS NO NEED FOR ANY SALT

(As the song grows faster, the CHILDREN's game grows wilder)

OH SHE MADE THE WATER HOT
SHE MADE THE WATER BOILING

SHE PUT IT IN THE POT
AND SHE STIRRED IT WITH THE SPOON

THEN SHE TOOK THE LITTLE BOY
AND CHOPPED HIM INTO PIECES
STUFFED HIM IN THE POT
TILL THERE WASN'T ANY ROOM

BUT MARLINCHEN STOOD BY
WEEPING AND WEEPING
THINKING IT WAS ALL HER FAULT
AND HER TEARS FELL INTO THE PAN SO THAT
THERE WAS NO NEED FOR ANY SALT!

(The VILLAGERS poke their heads in from the wings)

MARLINCHEN, VILLAGERS, CHILDREN

OH THE WATER IT GREW BLACK
THE WATER IT GREW BLACKER
BLACKER BLACKER BLACKER
BLACKER THAN THE NIGHT
(As the STEPMOTHER stirs faster and faster)
AND THE WATER IT GREW THICK
THICKER THICKER THICKER
BUT SHE STIRRED IT UP SO FAST
THAT THE SOUP CAME OUT JUST RIGHT

MARLINCHEN, VILLAGE CHILDREN

BUT MARLINCHEN STOOD BY
WEEPING AND WEEPING
THINKING IT WAS ALL HER FAULT
AND HER TEARS FELL FASTER AND FASTER AND FASTER
TILL THERE WAS NO NEED FOR ANY SALT
(Picking up speed)
AND HER TEARS FELL FASTER AND FASTER AND FASTER

TILL THERE WAS NO NEED FOR ANY SALT
(As the song reaches a crescendo and the CHILDREN jump higher and higher)
AND HER TEARS FELL FASTER AND FASTER AND FASTER
TILL THERE WAS NO NEED FOR ANY SALT!

(Light comes up on the HUSBAND)

HUSBAND

When I woke up, it was almost dark. I'd slept the entire afternoon! I was walking home, on my way through the woods, when —

(A pause)

These incredible — these *unbelievable* smells came from the house. She was of course a great cook, but this was like. . . *fantastic*. . . a fantastic aroma. It was very strange because I wasn't even *hungry*. But that smell came wafting out of the house and I felt like I had never eaten in my life! I remember my boots creaking faster and faster because I was just *dying* to have whatever that was! I rushed right in and sat down at the table and it was all *set*! *Beautifully*! Candlesticks and flowers and big white napkins and a white, white tablecloth.

(Another chord plays under)

Just like in my dream.

MARLINCHEN

(Rushing to him)

Daddy, Daddy, couldn't we go out to eat?

HUSBAND

What's your mother making?

MARLINCHEN

Soup.

(Desperate)

Couldn't we, Daddy?

HUSBAND

Who wants to go out when we can have that fabulous soup?

(Whipping the tablecloth off the table and wrapping it around his neck)
God, that *smell.*

MARLINCHEN
Don't do that, Daddy.

HUSBAND
What's happening with that soup? I've got to eat.

MARLINCHEN
I didn't do anything wrong, Daddy.

HUSBAND
I must eat. I must.

MARLINCHEN
I didn't do anything wrong.

HUSBAND
Marlinchen. Please.
(Calling into the kitchen)
BRING IN THE SOUP!

MARLINCHEN
(In a wail)
Daddy, Daddy, listen to me!
(Frantic, she climbs onto the table)
I didn't do anything wrong, okay?

HUSBAND
Marlinchen. Get off the table.

MARLINCHEN
(Getting off the table. Banging her fists down)
I want to go *out* to eat.

HUSBAND
Don't do that, Marlinchen.
(As she keeps banging the table)
STOP IT!

MARLINCHEN

(Chanting)

I want to go *out* to eat.
I want to go out,
I want to go out,
I want to go out to eat!

HUSBAND

(Overlapping, moaning)

Food, food. *Anything*!

(Resigned, MARLINCHEN goes over to the black pot and reluctantly brings it to her father, who waits impatiently, tapping his feet.

He takes a large spoonful of soup from the pot, tastes it)

HUSBAND

(Turning to us)

It was black. Blacker than anything you can imagine.

MARLINCHEN

It was the blood. That was what made it so black.

"Soup"

HUSBAND

SOUP
THIS IS SOUP
LIKE I'VE NEVER HAD
THE MORE I EAT IT
THE MORE I AM MAD FOR
THIS SOUP
WHAT A SOUP
A SPECTACULAR SOUP OF ALL TIME
AND I WON'T LET YOU TASTE IT
'CAUSE I DON'T WANT TO WASTE IT
FOR SOMEHOW IT FEELS LIKE IT'S MINE
MINE ALONE
RIGHT DOWN TO THE

BONES
THESE ARE BONES
LIKE I'VE NEVER SEEN
WHITE, EXQUISITE, IMPECCABLY CLEAN
OH THESE BONES
FUNNY BONES
THESE ARE BONES THAT WILL GO DOWN IN TIME
AND ALTHOUGH I'VE HAD PLENTY
MY BOWL SEEMS SO EMPTY
AND MY STOMACH HAS STARTED TO ROAR
I FEEL STUFFED
BUT STILL I WANT

MARLINCHEN

DIS-GUS-TING
DADDY THAT'S DISGUSTING
GET AWAY FROM ME
I DON'T WANT TO BE IN YOUR VICINITY
AND DON'T YOU EVER ASK ME TO SIT ON YOUR
KNEE
DISGUSTING DADDY

DADDY THAT'S DISGUSTING
WHAT IF SOMEONE SAW
THE WAY YOU CHEW THE BONES
THE WAY YOU GNAW AND GNAW
FOR DADDIES WHO DEVOUR
THERE SHOULD BE A LAW
PREVENTING DADDIES

FROM BURPING HERE
AND FROM SLURPING THERE
FROM EVEN GETTING IT IN THEIR HAIR
TONIGHT I PROMISE TO SAY A PRAYER
FOR MY POOR DADDY

HUSBAND

MORE
GIVE ME MORE

GIVE ME MORE MORE AND MORE
THE MORE I EAT IT
THE MORE I WANT MORE OF
THAT SOUP
SUCH A SOUP
NOT TO FINISH IT WOULD BE A CRIME
FOR IT FILLS ME WITH WONDER
IT MAKES ME FEEL YOUNGER
IT MAKES ME FEEL ALMOST DIVINE
I WANT MORE
I WANT WHAT IS

MARLINCHEN

DADDY THAT'S DISGUSTING
ALL YOUR TEETH ARE BLACK
I THOUGHT THAT ALL YOU WANTED
WAS A LITTLE SNACK
BUT NOW YOU LOOK SO STRANGE
I WANT MY DADDY BACK
WHO IS THIS DADDY?

A DADDY WHO BECOMES SO DEPRAVED
SHOULD BE LOCKED UP IN AN OLD DARK CAVE
AND NOT COME OUT TILL HE CAN BEHAVE
COME ON OUT DADDY!

(She tries to pull the pot away from him, but he clings to it tenaciously.

Grasping the other side, MARLINCHEN drags him across the floor, wrenches the pot away.

Coming up behind her, he waltzes her around the room, finally pulls the pot back)

HUSBAND

MINE
IT IS MINE
EVERY BIT OF IT MINE

MINE THIS MINUTE
FROM NOW ON, FOREVER
OH MINE
ONLY MINE
IT'S BEEN GIVEN TO ME AS A SIGN
AND YOU CAN'T HAVE ANY

MARLINCHEN

I don't want any.

HUSBAND

I WON'T LET YOU
HAVE ANY
NOT A SPOONFUL
WILL I LEAVE BEHIND
NOT A DROP
TILL ALL OF IT'S
I MIGHT POP
BUT ALL OF IT'S
I WON'T STOP
TILL ALL OF IT'S

MARLINCHEN

You threw all the bones on the floor, Daddy. You're the Daddy. You're not supposed to do that. Daddy's dirty. Really dirty. Daddy's filthy. Clean up, Daddy! I'll fix you up, Daddy! Daddy, you've had enough!

(Delirious, he rushes around offering the soup to MARLINCHEN, who turns away, nauseated, then to the audience, and finally drains the last dregs himself)

HUSBAND

MI-I-I-I-I-I
I-I-I-I-NE!

MI-I-I-I-NE!
MI-I-I-I-NE!

MARLINCHEN

DADDY YOU'RE DISGUSTING
DADDY
DADDY-O-O!
DADDY YOU'RE DISGUSTING
DADDY
DADDY-O-O!

HUSBAND

(Sighing, satisfied)

Now come and give Daddy a nice big hug.

MARLINCHEN

(Sickened)

BLECHHHH! DISGUSTING DADDY! BLACHHHHH!

(As the HUSBAND belches loudly, MARLINCHEN lets out a groan of revulsion, followed by the final chord of "Soup."

Light comes up on the STEPMOTHER)

STEPMOTHER

When I came into the dining room, I found Marlinchen sitting under the table counting all the bones. Putting them in neat little piles, lining them up, small to big — very carefully, very methodically. I yelled at her. I know I shouldn't have. But I was so afraid she'd let something slip. She ran up the stairs crying. I wanted to run after her and tell her I was sorry. I wanted to tell her it wasn't *her* fault. None of it was *her* fault. But I couldn't run after her and I couldn't tell her. You can't do that with a child. Once you've done it, you can't go back. It just confuses them. Anyway, five minutes later she came downstairs, walked right past me with her best silk handkerchief — the one I'd given her for her birthday.

HUSBAND

I don't know why my wife yelled at her like that. It wasn't as if she'd done anything wrong. Well. . . maybe she was hungry. My wife, I mean. After all, I'd eaten everybody's dinner! But I couldn't help it. It was just so *good.*

MARLINCHEN

When she yelled at me, I ran right up to my room. Because I knew — I just knew I had to do something with those bones. I mean I couldn't let her throw them in the garbage. Because then there'd be nothing left.

HUSBAND

(Smiling, contented)

I don't think I'll ever eat anything so good again in my life.

Where would I? No one makes food like that anymore.

(He and the STEPMOTHER go out)

MARLINCHEN

(In a rush)

So I went upstairs to my chest of drawers, and took my silk handkerchief out of the bottom drawer, and went downstairs again and didn't even look at her, not one look, and I got all the bones from under the table and tied them up, wrapped them up very carefully in my handkerchief, and she didn't say a word, not one word, though I knew she must have been really angry, because that was the handkerchief she'd given me for my birthday.

(She pauses)

And I thought about my birthday and how happy we'd all been together, and I knew I'd never have a birthday like that again. . . because he wouldn't be there. And that made me cry — all over those bones. "Tears of blood," I thought. "Tears of blood." And it sounded just like one of those crazy books she was always reading.

(Music of "Under The Juniper" begins)

And I went outside and laid the handkerchief and the bones under the juniper tree, because I knew that's where he'd want to be. And I wiped my tears away. And it was really weird. My hand was all covered with blood.

"Under The Juniper"

MARLINCHEN

AND THEN SHE LAY DOWN
AND THEN SHE LAY DOWN
UNDER THE JUNIPER
IN THE GREEN GRASS

AND THEN SHE LAY DOWN
AND THEN SHE LAY DOWN
UNDER THE JUNIPER TREE

AND SHE DIDN'T CRY
AND SHE DIDN'T CRY

UNDER THE JUNIPER
IN THE GREEN GRASS

AND SHE DIDN'T CRY
NO SHE DIDN'T CRY
UNDER THE JUNIPER TREE

(Light comes up on the VILLAGE CHILDREN)

MARLINCHEN, VILLAGE CHILDREN

THEN THE JUNIPER TREE BEGAN TO STIR
AND ITS BRANCHES PARTED ASUNDER
(As the VILLAGE CHILDREN clap once)
CLAPPING TOGETHER BACK AND FORTH
WITH A SOUND JUST LIKE THUNDER

AND AH, A MIST AROSE FROM THE TREE
IT ROSE UP HIGHER AND HIGHER
AND RIGHT IN THE CENTER OF THIS MIST
IT *BURNED* LIKE A FIRE!

AND A BEAUTIFUL BIRD FLEW OUT OF THE FIRE
SINGING MAGNIFICENTLY
AND HE FLEW HIGH UP IN THE AIR
HIGH ABOVE THE TREE

AND WHEN HE WAS GONE
OH WHEN HE WAS GONE
GONE WAS THE HANDKERCHIEF
GONE ALL THE BONES

AND THE MIST DISAPPEARED
THE MIST DISAPPEARED
AND THERE STOOD THE TREE SHE HAD KNOWN

AND THEN SHE STOOD UP
AND THEN SHE STOOD UP
UNDER THE JUNIPER
IN THE GREEN GRASS

AND THEN SHE COULD SMILE
AND THEN SHE COULD SMILE
UNDER THE JUNIPER
UNDER THE JUNIPER
UNDER THE JUNIPER TREE

(Light comes up on the HUSBAND and STEPMOTHER)

HUSBAND

And before I knew it —

STEPMOTHER

Before I knew it —

HUSBAND

Marlinchen was back.

STEPMOTHER

She came back, as if nothing had ever happened, as if everything were perfectly fine.

HUSBAND

And I was so glad to see her her old self again, because there was a moment I was really worried about her. But there she was, smiling, happy. And she sat down at the table —

STEPMOTHER

And could you believe it? She asked me for something to eat!

(As MARLINCHEN, the HUSBAND and STEPMOTHER go out, light comes up on the FIRST WIFE in the juniper tree)

"The Bird Flew Away"

FIRST WIFE

BUT THE BIRD FLEW AWAY
OH THE BIRD FLEW AWAY
AND HE FLEW SO HIGH
AND HE FLEW SO LONG

AND HE FLEW TILL HE CAME
TO THE GOLDSMITH'S HOUSE
AND UP ON THE ROOF
UP ON THE ROOF
UP ON THE ROOF
HE SANG HIS SONG

(Light comes up on the BIRD, formed by the BOY and both VILLAGE CHILDREN, who move and sing together)

"My Mother She Killed Me"

BIRD

MY MOTHER SHE KILLED ME
MY FATHER HE ATE ME
MY SISTER, LITTLE MARLINCHEN
GATHERED TOGETHER ALL MY BONES
TIED THEM IN A SILKEN HANDKERCHIEF
LAID THEM BENEATH THE JUNIPER TREE
KYWITT, KYWITT, WHAT A BEAUTIFUL BIRD AM I!
KYWITT, KYWITT, OH WHAT A BEAUTIFUL BIRD
OH WHAT A BEAUTIFUL BIRD AM I! AM I!

(Light comes up on the GOLDSMITH)

GOLDSMITH

It was a Sunday. And you know I don't usually like to work on a Sunday. You know what I mean. Sundays are sort of a sacred thing in our house. But that Sunday I couldn't resist. It was because of this golden chain I'd been making. I mean this thing was exquisite. It had become almost a kind of obsession for me. I hadn't even shown it to anybody. I kept it hidden in my workshop, and I'd sneak down there and work on it — sometimes in the middle of the night.

GOLDSMITH'S WIFE (Offstage)

For God's sake, Alfred — come back to bed!

GOLDSMITH

I hadn't even shown it to my wife. You know why? Because

I wanted to keep it for myself. I'd never made anything so beautiful in my life. And it was just kind of by an accident. I mean I'm good. I'm a good goldsmith. But let's face it — I'm not *that* good.

(He pauses)

Anyway, that Sunday, I'd slipped down to my workshop without my wife knowing, and set to work with a passion on that chain. I mean I'd really finished it a day or two before, but I kept on polishing it and polishing it, because after all what was I going to do with it? It's not the kind of thing a man like me would wear. I mean, like what would my wife say? And everyone else in this town?

GOLDSMITH'S WIFE (Offstage)

Alfred, what are you doing down there?

GOLDSMITH

Anyway, there I was polishing away when. . . suddenly this song hit me. I mean it really *hit* me. Some crazy bird sitting on top of the roof singing, 'My mother she killed me!' Now what kind of a song is that? I ran outside with the chain in my hand, and I was so excited I lost one of my slippers (I'd snuck downstairs in my slippers) — but I ran right into the middle of the street, because I just had to hear that song again. And the sun — I mean, what can I say — the sun shone so brightly it was as if the street were made of gold. And I looked up and saw that bird — and he really was something that bird, he really was spectacular — and I waited for him to repeat his song. And when he didn't — I mean he just stared back at me — I stood very calm and very still, although I was dying to hear it right away, and I said, 'Hey Bird, I'd sort of like to hear that song again.'

(He pauses)

I don't know why I felt so intimidated by that bird. There was just, I don't know, something intimidating about him. But I wanted to hear it so much I said, 'Look Bird! Just sing it for me. Just sing that song again — please!' And the bird said,

BIRD

I do not sing twice for nothing!

GOLDSMITH

And I don't know what made me do it, but I said, 'Hey look! I'll give you this, I'll give you my golden chain! I'll give it to you, Bird, if you just sing that song again.' And it didn't even hurt me when he came and took it in his right claw, because I knew, I absolutely knew, I'd been making it for him all along.

BIRD

(As the GOLDSMITH's WIFE runs out with the lost slipper and listens too)

MY MOTHER SHE KILLED ME
MY FATHER HE ATE ME
MY SISTER, LITTLE MARLINCHEN

FIRST WIFE

AND THE BIRD FLEW AWAY
OH THE BIRD FLEW AWAY
AND HE FLEW SO HIGH
AND HE FLEW SO LONG

AND HE FLEW TILL HE CAME
TO THE SHOEMAKER'S HOUSE
AND UP ON THE ROOF
UP ON THE ROOF
UP ON THE ROOF
HE SANG HIS SONG

BIRD

MY MOTHER SHE KILLED ME!

(Light comes up on the SHOEMAKER)

SHOEMAKER

I had a little girl. A pretty little girl. She made up songs which sounded like bells when she sang them. And for every pair of shoes I made, she made up a story and put it in her song.

(He pauses)

But one day it was as if the house grew too small for her and she ran outside to the garden to sing.

(He pauses)
But then the garden grew too small and she ran out barefoot to the meadows beyond.

(He pauses)
But the meadows couldn't contain her, and she ran barefoot up to the mountains.

(He pauses)
And when she came home, for she always came home, her feet were all battered and bruised.

(He pauses)
So I made a pair of shoes for my little girl. Red, red they were. Redder than the rocks at the mountain's edge.

(He pauses)
And when my child grew sick, and the whole house trembled from her trembling, I worked on those shoes night and day, day and night.

(He pauses)
And when I laid her in the earth and the world grew silent for me, so silent no sound would ever come into my mind, I put them high up on the shelf in my workroom and never looked at them again.

(He pauses)
That song was the first thing that entered my silence. I got up from my chair and went out into the garden. And when he flew toward me, I saw that his neck was gold and his feathers rainbows and his eyes stars. And I said softly, so softly, 'Ah bird, beautiful bird, won't you sing that song again?' And softly, so softly, he answered me.

BIRD

I do not sing twice for nothing.

SHOEMAKER

I took the shoes down from the shelf and dusted off the dust that had lain there for years, and polished the leather till it shown even redder than before. And when he swooped and snatched them from me and held them high in his left claw and stared at me with his great starry eyes, I was once more glad and the world all around me broke into sound.

BIRD

MY MOTHER SHE KILLED ME
MY FATHER HE ATE ME
MY SISTER, LITTLE MARLINCHEN

FIRST WIFE

AND THE BIRD FLEW AWAY
OH THE BIRD FLEW AWAY
AND HE FLEW SO HIGH
AND HE FLEW SO LONG

(As light comes up on the MILLER and the MILLER'S WIFE)

AND HE FLEW TILL HE CAME
TO A TUMBLEDOWN MILL
AND UP ON THE ROOF
UP ON THE ROOF
UP ON THE ROOF
HE SANG HIS SONG

MILLER

My wife and I were — we were —

MILLER'S WIFE

(Nudging him)

Shhh.

MILLER

We were just in the middle of —

MILLER'S WIFE

Henry.

MILLER

(As his WIFE tries to stop him)

I mean, it was *just* in the *middle*.

MILLER'S WIFE

Henry. Please.

MILLER

Anyway, that's not the point. *Literally* in the middle. . .

And then suddenly BOOM! '*My mother she killed me!*' That song totally distracted me.

MILLER'S WIFE

Totally.

MILLER

I tore myself out of her arms and ran outside with my pants falling down and my wife running behind me. And I ran straight to the mill because I just had to tell my men about this. I mean my men couldn't miss *this.*

(The other VILLAGERS appear, the two VILLAGE CHILDREN joining them)

MILLER

And there they were, all grinding away — fifteen men, hardest workers around — hewing this huge millstone. 'C'mon men, take a break! Don't you hear what I hear?'

BIRD

(Performed now by the BOY alone)

MY MOTHER SHE KILLED ME

MILLER

(Overlapping on "ME")

And one of my men stopped working.

BIRD

MY FATHER HE ATE ME

MILLER

(Overlapping on "ME")

And two more stopped working and listened to that.

BIRD

MY SISTER, LITTLE MARLINCHEN
GATHERED TOGETHER ALL MY BONES

MILLER

Then four more stopped —

BIRD

(Overlapping on "stopped")

TIED THEM IN A SILKEN HANDKERCHIEF

MILLER

Now only eight were hewing.

BIRD

LAID THEM BENEATH

MILLER

Now only five —

BIRD

THE JUNIPER TREE

MILLER

And now only one.

BIRD

KYWITT, KYWITT, WHAT A BEAUTIFUL BIRD AM I!
KYWITT, KYWITT, OH WHAT A BEAUTIFUL BIRD
OH WHAT A BEAUTIFUL BIRD AM I! AM I!

MILLER

(As the music continues under)

And then the last one stopped.

(A pause)

That bird. There he was looking at us, and we were looking at him. By God, he was beautiful. He was even more beautiful than my wife.

(Getting down on his knees)

Bird, please. Sing that song for us again.

(The music stops)

BIRD

I do not sing twice for nothing. Give me the millstone. Then I will sing it again.

MILLER

Yes, if it belonged to me only. Yes, you could have it. Certainly. Sure.

VILLAGERS, VILLAGE CHILDREN

Give it to him! If he sings it, give him anything. Anything for that song!

MILLER

(As the music begins under again)

And then all my millers set to work with a huge beam and raised up the stone. And it wasn't easy — believe me — but we got it up finally, we got it up! And then that bird zipped right down and stuck his neck through the hole. I mean he put that millstone on as if it were a collar.

(As a collective gasp bursts from the VILLAGERS and VILLAGE CHILDREN)

It was *amazing*! How he carried it I'll never know. But he flew right up to the top of the mill and we all listened and knew that never till our dying day would we ever hear anything like that bird's song again.

BIRD

MY MOTHER SHE KILLED ME
MY FATHER HE ATE ME
MY SISTER, LITTLE MARLINCHEN
GATHERED TOGETHER ALL MY BONES
TIED THEM IN A SILKEN HANDKERCHIEF
LAID THEM BENEATH THE JUNIPER TREE

(The FIRST WIFE appears, moves toward the BIRD, who kneels, facing out)

"He Was As Red As Blood (Reprise)"

FIRST WIFE

(Standing behind him)

AND IN HIS RIGHT CLAW THE CHAIN
IN HIS LEFT THE SHOES
IN HIS RIGHT CLAW THE CHAIN

IN HIS LEFT THE SHOES
AND THE GREAT STONE AROUND HIS NECK

FIRST WIFE and BIRD

THE MILLSTONE AROUND HIS NECK
WITH THE MILLSTONE AROUND HIS NECK
OH HE FLEW
HE FLEW

"The Bird Flew Away"

FIRST WIFE

(Lifting his arms)

AND HE SPREAD HIS GREAT WINGS
OH HE SPREAD HIS GREAT WINGS
AND HE FLEW SO HIGH
AND HE FLEW SO LONG
AND HE FLEW TILL HE CAME
TO HIS FATHER'S HOUSE. . .

(Light comes up on the HUSBAND, STEPMOTHER and MARLINCHEN)

HUSBAND

How happy I feel suddenly, how light-hearted! And there's a smell in the air, a smell just like cinnamon.

STEPMOTHER

Strange, I feel so uneasy. As if a great storm were coming.

BIRD

AND UP ON THE TREE

MARLINCHEN

Oh, I feel so good! I don't think I've ever felt this way before.

BIRD

ON THE JUNIPER TREE

STEPMOTHER

There's a fire in my veins, burning me, burning me.

BIRD

UP ON THE TREE
HE SANG HIS SONG

STEPMOTHER

Then I stopped my ears and I shut my eyes and I would not look and I would not listen.

BIRD

MY MOTHER SHE KILLED ME!

STEPMOTHER

Oh God, God, would that I were a thousand feet beneath the earth so as not to hear that!

BIRD

MY FATHER HE ATE ME!

HUSBAND

I'm going out. I've got to see that bird up close. And when I saw him —

(He stops)

There was something so familiar . . . as if I'd . . . I swear I'd seen that bird before! And I stood there . . . remembering the snow, and the horse, and her body lying beneath the juniper. And something dropped from his claw just then. I was about to duck, but he looked at me so kindly, so full of love, that I stood perfectly still. . . and felt something fall around my neck. It was a golden chain, a golden chain more beautiful than anything I had ever seen.

BIRD

MY SISTER, LITTLE MARLINCHEN
GATHERED TOGETHER ALL MY BONES

MARLINCHEN

Oooh, I'm going out to see that bird too!

BIRD

TIED THEM IN A SILKEN HANDKERCHIEF

MARLINCHEN

And then he threw those red slippers down to me —

BIRD

LAID THEM BENEATH THE JUNIPER TREE

MARLINCHEN

Right down to my feet!

BIRD

KYWITT, KYWITT, WHAT A BEAUTIFUL BIRD AM I!

MARLINCHEN

And I felt so happy.

BIRD

KYWITT! KYWITT!

MARLINCHEN

But it was much *more* than happy. I felt like — like I could fly!

BIRD

OH WHAT A BEAUTIFUL BIRD!
OH WHAT A BEAUTIFUL BIRD AM I! AM I!

MARLINCHEN

(Overlapping on "Am I!")

And I put on those red slippers and I *was* flying!

(Breathing in deep)

Now nothing. . . nothing bad will ever ever happen again.

STEPMOTHER

(Coming down to the edge of the stage)

Well. Well. Well. I don't know what there is to feel so happy about. How can you be happy when the world is coming to an end? Don't you feel it? Don't you?

(She pauses)

But I too will go out. For if he gave them something, wouldn't he give me something too?

(Another pause. In a rush)

And I went out, and heard above me the great flap —

(As the flute, violin and cello whir)

The whirring of wings, wings above me hitting me almost. And I looked up and saw his eyes. . . those huge eyes staring at me.

(A pause)

And I knew I had never gotten rid of him.

(Light comes up instantly on the VILLAGERS and VILLAGE CHILDREN)

"Under The Juniper" (Reprise)

VILLAGERS, VILLAGE CHILDREN

THEN THE JUNIPER TREE BEGAN TO STIR
AND ITS BRANCHES PARTED ASUNDER
(With a single resounding clap)
CLAPPING TOGETHER BACK AND FORTH
WITH A SOUND JUST LIKE THUNDER

AND AH! A MIST AROSE FROM THE TREE
IT ROSE UP HIGHER AND HIGHER
AND RIGHT IN THE CENTER OF THIS MIST
IT *BURNED* LIKE A FIRE!

AND THE BEAUTIFUL BIRD FLEW OUT OF THE FIRE
SINGING MAGNIFICENTLY

BIRD

(Circling the STEPMOTHER)

MY MOTHER SHE KILLED ME!

(In the shape of a great bird, the VILLAGERS and VILLAGE CHILDREN converge on the STEPMOTHER)

VILLAGERS, VILLAGE CHILDREN

(Leaping up in a single swift movement)

AND *CRASH!* THE STONE FELL ON HER HEAD
AND CRUSHED HER BENEATH THE TREE

(They swoop down on the STEPMOTHER, forcing her off, as light comes up on the FIRST WIFE)

FIRST WIFE

AND WHEN HE WAS GONE
AND WHEN HE WAS GONE
GONE WAS THE STEPMOTHER
GONE WAS THE STONE

FIRST WIFE and HUSBAND

AND THE MIST DISAPPEARED
THE MIST DISAPPEARED

FIRST WIFE, HUSBAND, MARLINCHEN

(As the BIRD changes back into the BOY again, trembling all over to find himself alive)

AND THERE LAY THE BOY
THEY HAD KNOWN

FIRST WIFE, HUSBAND, MARLINCHEN, VILLAGE CHILDREN

AND THEN HE STOOD UP

(MARLINCHEN rushes to embrace the BOY. They cling to each other, laughing, crying)

FIRST WIFE, HUSBAND, MARLINCHEN, VILLAGE CHILDREN

AND THEN HE STOOD UP
UNDER THE JUNIPER
IN THE GREEN GRASS

AND THEN HE STOOD UP
AND THEN HE STOOD UP
UNDER THE JUNIPER —

"Finale"

BOY

(To MARLINCHEN)

I NEVER HAD A NAME
MAYBE AT LAST I CAN
MAYBE NOW WITHIN ITS BRANCHES
I'LL UNDERSTAND

MARLINCHEN	**BOY**
YOU NEVER HAD A NAME	I NEVER HAD —
BUT I KNOW WITH ME	I KNOW WITH YOU
YOU CAN	I CAN
WE WON'T GIVE UP	DEEP WITHIN
UNTIL WE FIND IT	ITS BRANCHES
COME, TAKE MY HAND	I'LL UNDERSTAND

MARLINCHEN and BOY

WE WON'T GIVE UP UNTIL WE FIND IT
COME, TAKE MY —

FIRST WIFE, VILLAGERS, VILLAGE CHILDREN

AND THEN THEY JOINED HANDS
AND THEN THEY JOINED HANDS
UNDER THE JUNIPER
IN THE GREEN GRASS

(As the HUSBAND clasps the BOY and MARLINCHEN to him)

TOGETHER AGAIN
FOREVER AGAIN
UNDER THE JUNIPER —

FIRST WIFE

AND THEN THEY COULD SMILE
AND THEN THEY COULD LAUGH

FIRST WIFE, VILLAGERS, VILLAGE CHILDREN

UNDER THE JUNIPER
IN THE GREEN GRASS

FIRST WIFE
REMEMBER THE PAST

FIRST WIFE, VILLAGERS, VILLAGE CHILDREN
BUT LIVE! LIVE AT LAST
UNDER THE JUNIPER
UNDER THE JUNIPER
UNDER THE JUNIPER TREE

HUSBAND, FIRST WIFE, THE BOY, MARLINCHEN
(Quiet)
REMEMBER THE PAST
BUT LIVE! LIVE AT LAST

COMPANY
(A growing crescendo, as the BOY, MARLINCHEN and their father move to the tree)
UNDER THE JUNIPER
UNDER THE JUNIPER
UNDER THE JUNIPER TREE.

End of Play